SIMPLE ITALIAN COOKERY

ANTONIA ISOLA

APPLEWOOD BOOKS
Bedford, Massachusetts

Original copyright 1912 by Harper & Brothers.
This edition copyright ©2005 Applewood Books.

This cookbook has been reprinted in cooperation with the Culinary Trust, which is the philanthropic arm of the International Association of Culinary Professionals (IACP). The Trust celebrates the culinary past and future by funding educational and charitable programs related to the culinary industry (including scholarships for students and career professionals; library research and travel grants for food writers), cookbook preservation and restoration; and hunger alleviation. Tax-deductible gifts to the Culinary Trust should be sent to:

The Culinary Trust
304 West Liberty Street, Suite 201
Louisville, KY 40202
Web site: www.theculinarytrust.com
Phone: (502) 581-9786 x264

Thank you for purchasing an Applewood book. Applewood reprints America's lively classics—books from the past that are still of interest to modern readers. For a free copy of our current catalog, write to:

Applewood Books
P.O. Box 365
Bedford, MA 01730

ISBN: 1-55709-573-6

10 9 8 7 6 5 4 3 2 1

Introduction
by Robert W. Brower

Released by Harper & Brothers on February 15, 1912, *Simple Italian Cookery* by Antonia Isola is the first English language Italian cookbook published in America. As you can see from the facsimile edition you hold in your hand, *Simple Italian Cookery* is a collection of recipes. The book has no preface, no introduction, no explanatory text, and no information about the author. Unlike modern cookbooks which have introductory comments at the start of each chapter and headnotes or sidebars as commentary for each recipe, the recipes in *Simple Italian Cookery* stand unadorned and alone.

On the face of the first edition dust jacket, however, there is some secondary information about the book, in the form of the publisher's sales pitch. It states:

> This book of Italian recipes was compiled by an American who has lived much in Rome. Italian cookery is almost unknown in this country except to those who have traveled in Italy. A popular misconception of Italian diet is that it is composed chiefly of garlic and oil. Though the Italians are naturally a frugal race—a Venetian's form of invitation is, "Come, eat four grains of rice with me"—they are excellent cooks. This collection of recipes contains a few of the hundred ways for preparing "Neapolitan paste"—the general term

for the numerous varieties of macaroni, vermicelli, and spaghetti—and for delicious *risotti* (dishes of which the foundation is rice). Soups, meats, vegetables, and sweets are not neglected. The American housewife will discover how to vary the monotony of the weekly bill of fare.

The incorporation of some simple Italian dishes into the American diet was feasible because, at the turn of the century, Italian cooking had obtained a limited foothold in American cuisine and the market for an all-Italian cookbook was strong.

Italian Cookery in America Before 1912

Professional chefs had included Italian recipes in cookbooks published in America before 1912, but these recipes were often lost in the vast number of other recipes in the book. For example, Louis Eustache Audot's *French Domestic Cookery*,[1] translated and published by Harper & Brothers in 1846, contained 1,200 recipes. Of these, 48 were for Italian dishes. Audot included a detailed recipe for making ravioli which were then boiled in broth and served with grated cheese. In Charles Elmé Francatelli's *Modern Cook*,[2] published in Philadelphia in 1880 (from the 1855 ninth London edition), there were 1,462 recipes. The few Italian recipes in this book included Francatelli's version of ravioli served in broth and a layered and baked macaroni dish. Alessandro Filippini, a chef–manager at Delmonico's restaurant in New York, provided 1,550 recipes in his

1889 cookbook, *The Table*.[3] Filippini's Italian dishes included four recipes with spaghetti, five recipes for macaroni, a correct recipe for risotto à la Milanaise, and an instruction for serving mortadella as an hors d'oeuvres.

Women authors of smaller foreign or international cookbooks published in America before 1912 included some authentic regional Italian dishes in their collections. Helen Campbell (1893),[4] Lia Rand (1894),[5] L. L. McLaren (1904),[6] and Louise Rice (1911)[7] published traditional Italian recipes for ravioli, risotto, and polenta. Lia Rand provided detailed instructions for making a fresh pasta, *tagliarini*, which could be added to soup or used to line a mold and make an Italian timbale.[8]

Classic, turn-of-the-century, domestic science cookbooks written by cooking school teachers contained recipes which used dried pasta. In her *Boston Cook Book*,[9] Mary Lincoln had a section entitled "Macaroni, Spaghetti, and Vermicelli" and noted that "Risotti" was a dish demonstrated at her lecture on "Economical Dishes." In Sarah Rorer's *New Cook Book*,[10] there were more than twenty recipes for Italian pastes (dried pasta) and a suggestion: "At dinner the Italian pastes take the place of potatoes or rice...."

There were magazine articles promoting the benefits of incorporating Italian food into the American diet. For example, in a series of three articles in *Century Magazine* starting with "Ungastronomic America," Henry Finck criticized American food products and proposed that Americans experiment by incorporating "diverse [foreign] food flavors" into their diet.

Regarding Italian cuisine, like Mrs. Rorer, Henry Finck suggested: "In the average American household macaroni is far too seldom served. It might advantageously replace potatoes at one of the three meals."[11]

Finally, the United States Department of Agriculture published macaroni and Italian recipes in its bulletins as part of a decade long campaign to promote America's expanding durum wheat industry and to support the more than 150 American manufacturers of macaroni products.[12]

The publication of Italian recipes reflected the fact that Italian cooking was on the American radar screen. In addition to the availability of some Italian recipes, by 1912 there were many successful Italian restaurants promoting Italian cookery in America. In San Francisco, the Fior d'Italia, which opened in 1886 and survived the Great Fire and Earthquake of 1906, was going strong.[13] Other San Francisco Italian restaurants, Buon Gusto, Campi's, Gianduja, and Sanguinetti's, also reopened after the 1906 earthquake and fire.[14]

Thus, by 1912, the time was ripe for a comprehensive, all-Italian cookery book; compared to other ethnic cookery books, it was overdue.

The Respectable Foundation of "Simple Italian Cookery"

Simple Italian Cookery sold for 50 cents, net.[15] Harper & Brothers promoted it with several newspaper advertisements. An ad in the February 24, 1912, *New York Times* stated:

This book of Italian recipes was compiled by an expert. Though frugal, the Italians are excellent cooks and the American housekeeper will find many interesting suggestions for preparing all sorts of soups, meats, vegetables and sweets. The book shows that Italian cookery is far from being all "garlic and macaroni."

Antonia Isola, the expert mentioned in the ad, collected 130 recipes which she presented in ten different chapters: 1) Soups; 2) Macaroni and Other Pastes; 3) Rice, etc.; 4) Sauces: 5) Eggs; 6) Fish; 7) Vegetables; 8) Meats; 9) Salads; and 10) Desserts. Print reviews of *Simple Italian Cookery* were generally very positive. One reviewer recognized the unprecedented scope of the presentation:

> Antonia Isola's little book on "Italian Cookery" would have gained in interest had it been prefaced by a few pages summing up the gastronomic peculiarities of the people of her extraction. However, the professional cook or the mistress who does her own cooking and wisely craves variety, will soon discover from a perusal of the recipes given what are the national and local flavors of the peninsula which gives us the best macaronis and oils, and some of the best cheeses and wines. Not a few of the dishes described in these pages are international. In the second section, however, we plunge in *medias res*—the spaghetti, vermicelli, and other varieties of maccaroni, among which, strange

to say, the best of them all, the tagliatelli, is not mentioned. Equally Italian are the risotto and other rice dishes, the ravioli, the polenta, the gnocchi of farina or potato. Eggs, fishes, vegetables, meats, can be cooked in many tempting Italian ways by following the directions of the author. She also pays due attention to the national desserts, among which chestnuts figure so prominently and appetizingly.[16]

As with any collection of recipes, the recipes in *Simple Italian Cookery* come from several different sources. Although it is not within the scope of this Introduction to source every recipe in *Simple Italian Cookery*, it is useful to note an important part of its respectable foundation. One source, *Leaves from Our Tuscan Kitchen*, is an 1899 English language Italian cookbook printed in London. It is generally considered a culinary classic.

Leaves from Our Tuscan Kitchen is itself a collection of recipes. The recipes in this cookbook were compiled by Janet Ross, a famous Victorian British travel, history, and biography writer living just outside Florence. By 1911, when *Simple Italian Cookery* was written, *Leaves from Our Tuscan Kitchen* had been reprinted six times.[17] Some of the recipes in *Simple Italian Cookery* are identical to recipes in the 1908 edition of *Leaves from Our Tuscan Kitchen*.[18]

Other recipes in *Simple Italian Cookery* are Antonia Isola's translations of recipes found in Pellegrino Artusi's *La Scienza in cucina e l'Arte di mangiar bene* (*Science in the Kitchen and the Art of Eating Well*).

Artusi's book was published in 1891. By 1910, it had been reprinted fourteen times with numerous additions. In it, "[t]he culinary styles of the different parts of Italy were codified in carefully formulated recipes, then published and distributed all over the nation."[19] Many consider this significant "unifying" culinary work to be the most influential Italian language cookbook.

Janet Ross also used Pellegrino Artusi's book as a source for *Leaves from Our Tuscan Kitchen*. Consequently, some of the recipes in *Simple Italian Cookery* can be traced from Isola to Ross to Artusi. For example, Isola's "Spinach 'in riccioli'" came from Ross's "Spinach in Riccioli" which, in turn, was a translation of Artusi's *Frittata in riccioli per contorno*.

Because many of the recipes in Isola's 1912 cookbook are anchored in Artusi's 1891 cookbook, she uses an older culinary vocabulary. For example, consistent with hearth or wood stove cookery, Isola repeatedly tells the reader to keep a dish warm by putting it "onto the back of the stove."

Cooking from a historic cookbook with 1890's recipes can be a challenge. Old recipes often lack essential details about ingredients and procedures. These ambiguities force the cook to make unassisted decisions about important parts of the recipe. For any cook wanting to try recipes in Isola's collection, her simple recipes for rice with peas (p. 18) and polenta with chopped sausages (p. 24) are good starting points.

Rice with peas, the Venetian classic *risi e bisi*, is Isola's translation of Artusi's recipe for *risotto coi piselli*. First, you make a standard *risotto bianco*, a white risotto. When the risotto is cooked *al dente*, butter is added (*mantecatura*) and the risotto is kept warm. Peas are cooked in a flavored broth and then, with grated cheese, added to the risotto. By properly adjusting the amount of broth, the final dish becomes *all'onda*, a "wavy" texture midway between a thin soup and a thick risotto.[20]

Isola's polenta with chopped sausages is a predecessor of today's traditional Italian-American polenta lasagna. The polenta is cooked very stiff. It can be molded into a loaf using a buttered Pyrex bread pan, if you wish. While the polenta cools, a simple chopped sausage sauce is prepared. For the brand name "Deerfoot" sausages, try sweet or mild Italian pork sausage. After layering the polenta slices with the sausage sauce and grated cheese, briefly bake the dish in a warm oven.

Antonia Isola: "an American who has lived much in Rome"

A certain amount of mystery surrounds Antonia Isola, the author of *Simple Italian Cookery*. The first edition dust jacket identifies the author as "an American who has lived much in Rome." According to Kathryn Bitting, America's first cookbook bibliographer, Antonia Isola did not exist.[21] "Antonia Isola" was a pseudonym, an Italian *nom de plume* created by Harper and Brothers to sell an Italian cookbook.

The commercial use of an ethnic pseudonym to suggest authenticity is not unusual.[22] As a name, "Antonia Isola" suggests an ordinary Italian woman unlike the name of the actual author of *Simple Italian Cookery*, Miss Mabel Earl McGinnis.

Mabel Earl McGinnis was born on May 16, 1876, in New York, the last in a family of six children. Mabel's family was one of some consequence and affluence.[23]

Two of Mabel's sisters had significant and well-documented careers in the Arts. Adele Lydia McGinnis, a portrait painter, met Albert Herter, a muralist and a designer, in Paris where they were art students. They married in New York City in 1893. Mr. Herter was wealthy due to a large inheritance from his father. The Herter's lived on an estate in East Hampton, Long Island, and at El Mirasol, an estate–hotel in Santa Barbara. One of their children, Christian Archibald Herter, born in Paris in 1895, served two terms as Governor of Massachusetts and as Eisenhower's Secretary of State from 1959-1961.

Bessie Woodruff McGinnis was an acclaimed writer who also lived for an extended time in Paris. She was a contributor to *Harper's Magazine*, *Century Magazine*, the *Saturday Evening Post* and the *Ladies Home Journal*. She married John Van Vorst in 1899 just before he died. With her sister-in-law, Marie Van Vorst, Bessie wrote *The Woman Who Toils*, a 1903 expose of the conditions of the women who worked in American mills and factories.

Mabel and her sister Bessie were living with their mother in Paris when Lydia McGinnis unexpectedly died in March 1898. One friend wrote: "Tomorrow we are all going to the funeral and I dread it for all of them. I can hardly conceive a person worst fitted to stand the wear and tear than poor little supersensitive Mabel. I don't know at all what is to become of her now. . . . Fancy the horrible utter desolation of having your mother die in Paris and be cremated at Pere LaChaise with Carême and confetti rampaging round the streets. I am so sorry for her."[24] Shortly after the funeral, Mabel returned to New York. She lived with the Herters in East Hampton and worked as a designer and a painter.

After her father died in June 1901, Mabel traveled and lived in Italy. At one point, she was engaged "to a Sicilian, a bandit or something." Mabel ultimately settled in Rome, living at 88 Via Capo le Case. Via Capo le Case is a very short street in northeast Rome near the Piazza di Spagna, home of the Spanish Steps. At that time, one of the Anglo-American communities in Rome occupied that neighborhood: "There is nothing more endearing than the sight of a roomful of English people at their afternoon tea in a strange land."[25]

Mabel's contract with Harper and Brothers to write *Simple Italian Cookery* was signed on March 18, 1911, while she was living at 88 Via Capo le Case. Her compensation was 5 cents per book after the sale of 1,000 copies.[26] The circumstances of her obtaining this contract are unknown. Since she knew several writers with Harper and Brothers, including her sister Bessie, her sister-in-law Marie Van Vorst, and her friend W. D. Howells, it is likely the job came by way of referral.

Mabel's life dramatically changed when she met Norval Richardson, the Second Secretary of the American Embassy in Rome. Born in Vicksburg, Mississippi, in 1877, Norval Richardson was a career diplomat. After serving as Second Secretary in Havana from 1909 to 1911 and at Copenhagen from 1911 to 1913, Norval arrived in Rome, December 1913. He took over as Secretary of the Embassy in 1916.

Mabel and Norval were married on January 6, 1917. The wedding took place in the Palazzo del Drago, the Ambassador of Rome's residence. The Ambassador and the Embassy staff attended as well as the Mayor of Rome. Five years after the publication of *Simple Italian Cookery*, Mabel Earl McGinnis became Mrs. Norval Richardson, a diplomat's wife.

While in Rome, the Richardsons had one daughter, Anne.

After serving in Rome until 1920, Norval Richardson was assigned to the American embassies in Chile, Portugal and Japan. Richardson retired from the diplomatic service in 1924.

The Richardson family lived in France and Italy for several years before building a home in Gstaad, Switzerland. For financial reasons, they rented out their Gstaad home and moved to Dinard, France.

During his retirement, Norval Richardson wrote numerous books, including one on his diplomatic service. He died in Bermuda on October 22, 1940.

The place and date of death of Mabel McGinnis is unknown.

© 2005 by Robert W. Brower

Notes

1. Audot, Louis Eustache. *French Domestic Cookery, Combining Elegance With Economy; Describing New Culinary Implements And Processes; The Management of the Table; Instructions for Carving; French, German, Polish, Spanish, and Italian Cookery; In Twelve Hundred Receipts.* New York: Harper & Brothers, 1846. 340 p.
2. Francatelli, Charles Elmé. *The Modern Cook; A Practical Guide to the Culinary Art in All its Branches, Comprising, in Addition to English Cookery, the Most Approved and Recherché Systems of French, Italian, and German Cookery; Adapted as Well for the Largest Establishments as for the Use of Private Families.* Philadelphia: T.B. Peterson and Brothers, no date. 585 p. The twenty-sixth London edition of Francatelli's book was reprinted in Philadelphia in 1895 by David McKay, publisher. For this edition, the text on the title page was expanded to read: "Adapted for the use of all Families, large or small, as well as for Hotels, Restaurants, Cooks, Cake Bakers, Clubs and Boarding Houses; in fact, for all places wherever Cooking is required, while at the same time, all will save money by referring to its pages."
3. Filippini, Alessandro. *The Table: How to Buy Food, How to Cook It, and How to Serve It.* New York: Charles L. Webster & Company, 1889. Revised edition with supplements, 1890. 505 p. After a trip around the world in 1902, Filippini prepared a massive international cookbook containing 3,325 numbered recipes. This book contained spaghetti and macaroni dishes, a recipe for risotto Piedmontaise, and a recipe for "Gnocchis, Italienne." *The International Cook Book. Over 3,300 Recipes gathered from all over the World, including many never before published in English.* New York: Doubleday, Page & Company, 1906. 1,059 pages.

4. Campbell, Helen (Stuart). *In Foreign Kitchens: With Choice Recipes from England, France, Germany, Italy, and the North.* Boston: Roberts Brothers, 1893. 114 p.

5. Rand, Lia. *The Philosophy of Cooking: Comprising Forty-One Explanatory Letters and Three Hundred and Ten Foreign Recipes, French, German and Italian, Adapted for the American Home Table.* Brooklyn: Published for the Author (W. Headrich, Printer), 1894. 196 p.

6. McLaren, L. L. *High Living; Recipes From Southern Climes.* San Francisco: Paul Elder and Co., 1904. 61 p.

7. Rice, Louise. *Dainty Dishes from Foreign Lands.* Chicago: A. C. McClurg & Co., 1911. 58 p.

8. There were 22 Italian recipes in an anonymous collection of 365 international recipes, presumably selected from Mrs. Lemcke, *Table Talk*, *Boston Cooking School Magazine* and others. *365 Foreign Dishes. A Foreign Dish for every day of the year.* Philadelphia: George W. Jacobs & Co., 1908. 154 p.

9. Lincoln, Mary Johnson. *Mrs. Lincoln's Boston Cook Book. What to Do and What Not to Do in Cooking.* Boston: Roberts Brothers, 1884. 536 pages.

10. Rorer, Sarah Tyson. *Mrs. Rorer's New Cook Book. A Manual of Housekeeping.* Philadelphia: Arnold and Co., 1898. 731 p.

11. Finck, Henry T. "Ungastronomic America, With a Theory of Wholesome Eating; Multiplying the Pleasures of the Table; The Future of Cooking and Eating," *Century Magazine*, November and December 1911, January 1912, Vol. LXXXIII, Nos. 1, 2, and 3, pp. 28-36, 220-228, 439-448.

12. America's durum wheat crop survived the black rust epidemic of 1904 when other wheat varieties died. As durum wheat production skyrocketed, the quality of American manufactured dried pasta improved making it as good as, or better than, imported Italian pasta. This, in turn, lead to a call for American cooks to use more American-made macaroni. de Kruif, Paul. *Hunger Fighters.* New York: Harcourt, Brace and Co., 1928, pp. 3-30.

13. Brevetti, Francis. *The Fabulous Fior—Over 100 Years In An Italian Kitchen. The History of San Francisco's Fior d'Italia, America's Oldest Italian Restaurant, Established 1886*. Nevada City, CA: San Francisco Bay Books, 2004. 166 p.
14. Edwords, Clarence E. *Bohemian San Francisco: Its Restaurants and Their Most Famous Recipes. The Elegant Art of Dining*. San Francisco: Paul Elder and Co., 1914. 138 p.
15. "Net" means net to the publisher. Retail price varied. In February 1924, for example, as part of "The World Cook" cookbook promotion, R. H. Macy & Co. advertised *Simple Italian Cookery* for sale at 81 cents.
16. "Simple Italian Cookery" [Book review.] *Nation*, Vol. 94, June 20, 1912, p. 620. The tagliatelle recipe was not entirely omitted. Isola called her "homemade" fresh pasta, i.e., *pasta fatta in casa*, "ribbon" macaroni.
17. Ross, Janet. *Leaves from Our Tuscan Kitchen or How to Cook Vegetables*. London: J. M. Dent, 1899. 168 p. The first edition had 362 recipes nominally devoted exclusively to Tuscan vegetable cookery. It was reprinted three times. For the fifth printing in 1908, Ross provided 43 additional recipes. The 1908 fifth edition was reprinted in 1911, 1914, 1919, 1927, 1931 and 1936.
18. The similarity between some of the recipes in *Simple Italian Cookery* and those in *Leaves from Our Tuscan Kitchen* was first noted by Johan Mathieson, a used cookbook dealer in Portland, Oregon. Copying these recipes was not plagiarism; *Leaves from Our Tuscan Kitchen* was not copyright. In addition, most of its recipes were just translations from French or Italian sources. See, Bugialli, Giuliano. *The Fine Art of Italian Cooking*. New York: Times Books, 1977, at Preface, xiv. But unlike *Leaves from Our Tuscan Kitchen*, there are no overtly French recipes in *Simple Italian Cookery*.
19. Camporesi, Piero. (translated by Joan Krakover Hall.) *The Magic Harvest. Food, Folklore and Society*. Cambridge, MA: Polity Press, 1993, p. 115.

20. To learn more about *risi e bisi*, see, "Rice and Peas: A Preface with Recipes" in Thorne, John, *Simple Cooking*, New York; Viking, 1987, pp. xi-xxix.
21. Bitting, Katherine Golden. *Gastronomic Bibliography*. San Francisco, 1939, p. 242.
22. Griffin, Robert J. (ed.) *The Faces of Anonymity: Anonymous and Pseudonymous Publication from the Sixteenth to the Twentieth Century*. New York: Palgrave Macmillan, 2003.
23. Mabel's father, John McGinnis Jr., was born in New Jersey in 1831, but by 1850 he had moved to Joliet, Illinois, and was working in a bank. Mabel's mother, Lydia Olivia Matteson, was born in Joliet in 1837. Lydia's father was elected Governor of Illinois in 1852, whereupon the Matteson family moved from Joliet to Springfield.

    John McGinnis married Lydia Matteson in Springfield in 1856. After moving to Quincy, Illinois, John became the president of the Bank of Quincy. The McGinnis family moved from Quincy to Chicago to New York City in the late 1860s where John continued to work as a banker and then as a broker. At that time, the McGinnis family was affluent: the McGinnis children had a governess from France and the family had three domestic servants.

    Sterling, Albert Mack. *The Sterling Genealogy*. New York: The Grafton Press, 1909.
24. Emmet, Lydia Field. Personal letter to Jane Emmet, March 18, 1898. Emmet Family papers, 1792-1989. Available on microfilm, Archives of American Art, Smithsonian Institution, Washington, D.C. 20560.
25. For a description of this neighborhood and its inhabitants, see Howells, W. D. *Roman Holidays and Others*, New York; Harper and Brothers, 1908, Chap. VI, sec. IV, "The Anglo-American Neighborhood of the Spanish Steps," pp. 98-110.
26. There was a separate royalty for copies sold in Europe. Antonia Isola's book was popular; sales passed 1,000 in May 1912. The book was also reprinted several times.

CONTENTS

	PAGE
Soups	3
Macaroni and other Pastes	9
Rice, Etc.	18
Sauces	29
Eggs	35
Fish	39
Vegetables	42
Meats	51
Salads	58
Desserts	60
Index	63

SIMPLE ITALIAN
COOKERY

SIMPLE ITALIAN COOKERY

SOUPS

Beef Soup Stock
(*Brodo di Carne*)

- 1 pound of round of beef
- 2 quarts of water
- 2 small, new carrots, or ½ of an old carrot
- ½ pound of beef bones
- 2 small potatoes
- 1 onion
- 1 tomato, fresh or canned
- Parsley

Boil the beef, bones, and vegetables in two quarts of water over a slow fire—adding pepper and salt. Skim occasionally, and after two hours add two tablespoons of sherry; then strain through fine soup-strainer or cheese-cloth. This is the basis of all the following soups, except when otherwise stated.

To make this stock richer, add a turkey leg to above receipt; boil one and a half hours, then add one-half a pound of finely chopped beef. Cook for half an hour longer, then strain.

To make meat jelly, add a little gelatine to the soup stock five minutes before straining.

SIMPLE ITALIAN COOKERY

To give a good dark color to the stock, add a few drops of "caramel," which is prepared in the following manner:

Put three tablespoons of granulated sugar into a saucepan with a little water, and until the sugar has become dark and reddish; then add a little more water and boil again until the sugar is melted. Strain and pour into a bottle when the caramel will keep perfectly for several weeks.

Chicken Broth
(*Brodo di Capone*)

This is made like the meat stock, substituting a fowl in place of the beef and bones.

Rice Soup
(*Minestra di Riso*)

Meat stock   2 tablespoons of rice

Cover the rice with water and boil for ten minutes; then drain and add to the stock (after it has been strained), and boil for five or ten minutes more.

Stracciatella Soup
(*Minestra di Stracciatella*)

1 egg   1 tablespoon bread crumbs
½ tablespoon of Parmesan cheese

Beat the egg, yolk and white together; add salt and the cheese, grated, and the bread crumbs; mix well together and add to the boiling stock (strained). Stir well with a fork to prevent the egg from setting, and boil for four or five minutes.

SOUPS

Vegetable Chowder
(*Minestrone alla Milanese*)

½ quart of stock	1 cup of rice
2 slices of lean pork, or a ham bone	2 tablespoons of dried beans
2 tomatoes, fresh or canned	1 tablespoon of peas, fresh or canned
2 onions	

Put into the stock the slices of pork, cut into small pieces; or, if desired, a ham bone may be substituted for the pork. Add the tomatoes, cut into small pieces also, the onions, in small pieces, and the rice. Boil all together until the rice is cooked. Then add the beans and the peas and cook a little longer. The soup is ready when it is thick. If desired, this chowder can be made with fish broth instead of the stock, and with the addition of shrimps which have been taken from their shells.

This dish can be served hot or cold.

Fish Broth
(*Brodo di Pesce*)

1 liberal pound of fresh codfish, or any other lean fish for boiling	1 quart of water 1 onion Parsley Salt and pepper

Boil until fish is thoroughly cooked; **strain and serve.**

Codfish Soup
(*Zuppa di Merluzzo*)

Take one-half pound of salt codfish that has been soaked, cut it up into squares, but not small.

Prepare in a saucepan four tablespoons of good olive-

SIMPLE ITALIAN COOKERY

oil, and one small onion cut into pieces. Cook the onion in the oil over a slow fire, without allowing the onion to become colored, then add a small bunch of parsley stems, a small piece of celery, a bay-leaf, and a small sprig of thyme. Cool for a few moments, then add two tomatoes, skinned and with the seeds removed, and cut into slices, two tablespoons of dry white wine, and one medium-sized potato, peeled and cut into slices, and, lastly, one cup of water.

When the potato is half cooked, add the codfish, then one-half tablespoon more of olive-oil. Remove the parsley stems, and put in instead one-half tablespoon of chopped-up parsley; add a good pinch of pepper, and some salt, if needed. When the vegetables are thoroughly cooked pour the soup over pieces of toasted or fried bread, and serve.

Lentil Soup
(*Brodo di Lenticchie*)

3 tablespoons of dried lentils	½ tablespoon of butter
	2 tablespoons of cream
Meat stock	

Cover the lentils with water and boil until they are quite soft. Pass them through a colander or a sieve. Melt the butter in a saucepan, add the lentils and cream, mixing well, then add a ladleful of the stock, and boil for a few minutes; then add the rest of the desired amount of stock, a ladleful at a time.

Vegetable Soup
(*Zuppa alla Primaverile*)

Take some cabbage, carrots, celery, onions, turnips, lettuce, squash, potatoes, beans, and peas. Chop each into very small pieces, wash and drain. Take a sauce-

SOUPS

pan, put in a heaping tablespoon of butter; chop up another small piece of onion and add to butter and fry until onion is golden; then add all the vegetables, salt, and pepper, and cover the saucepan. When the vegetables are half cooked, and their juice has become absorbed, dissolve one tablespoon of tomato paste in one-third of a cup of hot water, and add. Instead of the tomato paste there may be added to the onion, before putting in the vegetables, one tomato, peeled and cut into small pieces. When the tomato is cooked add the vegetables. Then add water, a little at a time, until you have sufficient quantity for two persons. Take a slice of bread and cut into small squares or diamonds—toast or fry as desired—put these into the soup plates, and pour the soup (without straining) over them.

Lettuce Soup
(*Zuppa di Lattuga*)

1 small lettuce	2 tablespoons of peas, fresh or canned
Meat stock	
2 potatoes	1 heaping tablespoon of flour
The leaves of a head of celery	

Put the potatoes, cold boiled, into the stock when it boils, add the celery leaves, the lettuce chopped up, the peas, and the flour mixed well with a little cold stock or water. Boil for one hour and a half, and serve with little squares of fried bread.

Pumpkin Soup
(*Zuppa di Zucca*)

1 slice of pumpkin	½ cup of water
2 tablespoons of butter	1½ cups of milk
1 tablespoon of sugar	

SIMPLE ITALIAN COOKERY

Peel the pumpkin and remove the seeds, cut into small pieces, and put into a saucepan with the butter, the sugar, a pinch of salt, and the water. Boil for two hours, then drain and put back into the saucepan with the milk, which has been boiled. Allow it to come to a boil, and then serve it with squares of fried bread.

Potato Soup
(*Zuppa alla Provinciale*)

2 large potatoes	2 tablespoons of butter
3 tablespoons of cream or milk	2 yolks of eggs
	Soup stock

Boil the potatoes, then rub them through a sieve. Put them into a saucepan with the butter, a little salt, and the cream or milk. Simmer until it is thick, then add the yolks of the two eggs to form it into a paste. Turn out onto the bread-board, cut into small dice, and throw them into the stock, which must be boiling. If desired, before serving sprinkle a little Parmesan cheese into the soup.

MACARONI AND OTHER PASTES

Macaroni with Tomato Sauce
(*Maccheroni al Sugo*)

2 quarts of water   ¾ pound of macaroni

Boil the water until it makes big bubbles. Add salt, then break the macaroni and put it in. Cover the saucepan and boil for fifteen minutes. The saucepan should not be too small, otherwise the macaroni will stick to the bottom.

Prepare the sauce as follows:

Take a good slice of ham fat, and chop very fine with it a piece of onion, a piece of celery, and some parsley. Then put this into a frying-pan and cook until the grease is colored. (If desired, add a small lump of butter.) When well colored add two tablespoons of tomato paste dissolved in a little hot water. Boil all together for fifteen minutes.

Drain the macaroni, and put it into the frying-pan with the sauce, mix well with fork and spoon over the fire, so that the macaroni will be thoroughly seasoned, then add three tablespoons of grated Parmesan cheese, mix again, and serve.

If no tomato paste is available make the tomato sauce as follows:

Chop up fine one-quarter of an onion, a piece of celery the length of a finger, two or three basil-leaves.

SIMPLE ITALIAN COOKERY

and a small bunch of parsley. Slice seven or eight tomatoes (fresh or canned), add salt and pepper, and put all on together to cook in four tablespoons of good olive-oil. Stir occasionally, and when it becomes as thick as cream, strain, and add the macaroni as before directed.

Macaroni with Meat and Sauce
(*Maccheroni al sugo di Carne*)

Take one-half pound of beef without fat. Prepare the ham fat as in the preceding receipt, chopped up with onion, celery, and parsley. Cut the meat into several pieces, put it with the fat, etc., into a frying-pan. Add salt and pepper. Cook until the meat is colored, then add two tablespoons of wine, white or red. When the wine is absorbed add two tablespoons of tomato paste dissolved in hot water. (Or tomato sauce as in preceding.) Boil all together for five minutes, with cover on the saucepan, then add one cup of boiling water, and allow it to simmer until the meat is thoroughly cooked—about one-half an hour. Boil and strain the macaroni as before, and pour over it the sauce from the meat. Mix well, and serve with the meat in the middle and the macaroni around it, with cheese (grated Parmesan) sprinkled over it.

This dish can be made with veal or mutton instead of the beef.

Macaroni with Butter and Cheese
(*Maccheroni al Burro*)

Boil and drain the macaroni. Take four tablespoons of table-butter, three tablespoons of grated Parmesan cheese, add to the macaroni in the saucepan, mix well over the fire, and serve.

MACARONI AND OTHER PASTES

Sicilian Macaroni with Eggplant

Slice one eggplant and put it under a weighted plate to extract the bitter juices. Then fry the slices delicately in lard. Make a ragout of chickens' hearts and livers as follows: Put two tablespoons of butter into a saucepan, fry the hearts and livers, and when cooked add two tablespoons of tomato paste, thinned with hot water (or a corresponding amount of tomato sauce). Cook for fifteen minutes.

Prepare three-quarters of a pound of macaroni, boiled and drained, then put it into the saucepan with the hearts and livers, add the eggplant and three tablespoons of grated Parmesan cheese. Mix well together and serve.

Vermicelli with Olive-oil and Anchovies

Take one-half pound of vermicelli, boil in salted water and drain. While boiling put into a saucepan three anchovies, cut up fine, with four tablespoons of olive-oil. Fry the anchovies in the oil, then put the vermicelli into the saucepan, mix well for a few moments on the fire, then serve.

Vermicelli with Olive-oil, Olives, Capers, and Anchovies

Take one-half pound of vermicelli and cover it well with salted water. Cook for about ten minutes. While it is boiling put into a saucepan four tablespoons of olive-oil, three anchovies cut up fine with six olives (ripe ones preferable) and one-half tablespoon of capers. When these are fried add the vermicelli (well drained), mix well, and put the saucepan at the back of the stove. Turn the vermicelli over with a fork every few minutes until it is thoroughly cooked.

Vermicelli with Fish

Boil one-half pound of vermicelli in salted water, drain, and mix with two tablespoons of olive-oil and a little chopped-up parsley. Then set to one side to get cool.

Take five smelts, split them, take out the bones, and fry them slightly in one teaspoon of olive-oil.

Butter a pan and sprinkle it with bread crumbs. Then put into it one-half of the cold vermicelli. Pour over this some thick tomato sauce (one tablespoon of tomato paste cooked in two tablespoons of olive-oil). Then put in the smelts cut in two, some anchovy, a few capers, and three or four ripe olives chopped up with one mushroom. Then add the rest of the tomato sauce, then the other half of the vermicelli, and on top a layer of bread crumbs. Season all well with salt and pepper. Put the pan into a moderate oven, and cook about an hour and a quarter, adding a little olive-oil when necessary, so that it will not dry up too much.

Any fish may be used instead of the smelts, cutting it into thin strips.

Spaghetti with Tunny-fish

While one-half pound of spaghetti is boiling in salted water prepare the following: Take two ounces of tunny-fish and cut them into small pieces. Put them into a saucepan and fry them in their own oil. This oil is generally sufficient, but should it not be, add another tablespoon of olive-oil. When the tunny have been fried add a teaspoonful of chopped parsley and four tomatoes, peeled and the seeds removed, and a pinch of pepper. Let the tomatoes cook thoroughly. When they are cooked put the spaghetti into the

MACARONI AND OTHER PASTES

saucepan and move them about with a fork and spoon until they are thoroughly mixed with the sauce and the tunny. Then serve.

Timbale of Vermicelli with Tomatoes
(Neapolitan Receipt)

Take ten medium-sized fresh tomatoes and cut them in two crosswise. Put a layer of these into a baking-dish with the liquid side touching the bottom of the dish. Now put another layer with the liquid side up, sprinkle on salt and pepper. Break the raw vermicelli the length of the baking-dish and put a layer of it on top of the tomatoes. Now add another layer of the tomatoes, with the skin side touching the vermicelli, a second layer with the liquid side up, salt and pepper, and another layer of the raw vermicelli, and so on, the top layer being of tomatoes with their liquid side touching the vermicelli. Heat three or four tablespoons of good lard (or butter), and when the lard boils pour it over the tomatoes and vermicelli; then put the dish into the oven and cook until the vermicelli is thoroughly done. After cooling a little while, turn it out into a platter.

Macaroni "alla San Giovannello"

While three-quarters of a pound of macaroni are boiling in salted water prepare the following: Chop up fine two ounces of ham fat with a little parsley. Peel six medium-sized tomatoes, cut them open, remove the seeds, and any hard or unripe parts, and put them on one side. Take a frying-pan and put into it one scant tablespoon of butter and the chopped ham fat. When the grease is colored put in the sliced tomatoes with salt and pepper. When the tomatoes are cooked and begin to sputter put the macaroni into the pan with them, mix well, add grated Parmesan cheese, and serve.

Ribbon Macaroni

(*Pasta fatta in Casa. Fettuccini*)

2½ cups of flour
2 eggs
3 tablespoons of cold water
½ teaspoon of salt

Put the flour on a bread-board. Make a hole in the middle of it, and break the eggs into it. Add the water and the salt, and mix all together with a fork until the flour is all absorbed and you have a paste which you can roll out. Then take a rolling-pin and roll it out very thin, about the thickness of a ten-cent piece. Leave it spread out like this until it has dried a little. Then double it over a number of times, always lengthwise, and cut it across in strips about one-half inch wide. Boil two quarts of salted water, and put the ribbons into it, and cook for ten minutes, then drain. Serve with the meat and sauce as in receipt for Macaroni with Meat and Sauce, or with the tomato sauce and cheese only, as desired.

Ravioli with Meat

Prepare the paste as in the preceding receipt.

Take whatever meat is desired—chicken, turkey, or veal—this must always be cooked. (Left-over meat may be utilized this way.) Chop the meat very fine, add one tablespoon of grated Parmesan cheese, one egg, a dash of nutmeg, a dash of grated lemon-peel, one tablespoon of butter, cold. Mix these ingredients in a bowl. Take a teaspoon of the mixture and put it into the extended paste, about two inches from the edge.

MACARONI AND OTHER PASTES

Take another spoonful and put it about two inches away from the first spoonful. Continue to do this until you have a row of teaspoonfuls across the paste. Then fold over the edge of the paste so as to cover the spoonfuls of mixture, and cut across the paste at the bottom of them. Then cut into squares with the meat in the middle of each square; press down the paste a little at the edges so the meat cannot fall out. Continue to do this until all the meat and the paste are used up.

Put the little squares of paste and meat into the boiling salted water a few at a time, and boil for ten minutes. Serve with tomato sauce, or butter and grated Parmesan cheese.

Ravioli with Brains

Take one lamb's brains and parboil in slightly salted water for five minutes. Put into a bowl with a small quantity of curds, one egg, salt and pepper, dash of nutmeg, and a little grated Parmesan cheese, and mix all together. Then put by teaspoonfuls on the paste as in preceding receipt. Cook for ten minutes in boiling salted water, and serve with tomato sauce.

Ravioli of Curds and Spinach

1 small bunch of spinach   ½ pound of curds

Cook the spinach, drain, and chop up fine, add the curds, one egg, salt and pepper, dash of nutmeg, and a little grated cheese. Add to the paste, and boil as before.

Sweet Ravioli
(Ravioli Dolce)

These ravioli can be used also as a dessert by preparing them as follows:

SIMPLE ITALIAN COOKERY

Take ½ pound of flour   1 tablespoon of butter
2 tablespoons of lard

Work this into a paste and roll out thin.

Take one-half pound of curds, add one egg, and the yolk of a second egg, two tablespoons of granulated sugar, a few drops of extract of vanilla. Mix well together and add to the paste as before. Then fry in lard until a golden brown. Serve with powdered sugar.

Timbale of Macaroni

Take a small piece of ham fat, one-half of onion, piece of celery, parsley, small piece of carrot. Chop up fine together. Put into a saucepan, and when the vegetables are fried add two or three mushrooms which have been chopped fine; after five minutes add two tablespoons of tomato paste, thinned with five tablespoons of hot water (or equal quantity of tomato sauce without water). When the sauce is cooked take out the mushrooms and put them on one side.

Take one-half pound of macaroni. Boil in salted water for fifteen minutes, drain, and add the sauce described above. Add two tablespoons Parmesan cheese, grated, and one tablespoon of butter.

Butter well a mold, then cover with a thin layer of bread crumbs the bottom and sides. Pour into the mold one-half the macaroni, then place on it a layer of mushrooms which you have taken out of the sauce. Now add the other half of the macaroni, and then another thin layer of bread crumbs. Put the mold into the oven without turning it over, and bake in a slow oven until well browned. Then turn out and serve.

To this timbale, if desired for variety, cold meat of any kind cut up fine may be added to the sauce; and

MACARONI AND OTHER PASTES

one egg, hard boiled, and cut into four pieces. Add the egg, and the pieces of meat which you have removed from the sauce, to the timbale at the same time that you add the mushrooms.

Rice Timbale

This timbale is made in the same way as the preceding one, only substituting rice for macaroni. One-half cup of rice.

Timbale of Ribbon Macaroni

This is prepared as the two preceding ones, using Ribbon Macaroni instead of rice or ordinary macaroni.

RICE, ETC.

Rice with Peas

½ cup of rice	2 tablespoons of butter
Grated Parmesan cheese	1 small onion

Chop the onion up fine and put it into the saucepan with one-half the butter (one tablespoon). Cook until the onion is brown, then pour on the rice (raw) and fry until the rice is dry. Then add hot water, a ladleful at a time, taking care not to let the rice boil too hard, as it will then become hard in the middle and floury around the edges. When the rice is cooked, put the saucepan at the back of the stove, and add the rest of the butter. Before taking off the stove add a little grated Parmesan cheese and the peas, which have been prepared as follows:

Take a small piece of ham fat, one-half small onion, and some parsley. Chop together fine, add three tablespoons of olive-oil, salt and pepper, and put into a saucepan on the fire. When the onion is colored add one can of green peas (or fresh peas, according to season). When the peas have absorbed all the olive-oil add a sufficient quantity of broth to cover them (or water) and cook until peas are soft. Then mix the peas with the rice, add one tablespoon of Parmesan cheese, and serve.

RICE, ETC.

Rice "alla Romana"
(Risotto alla Romana)

A small piece of ham fat	1 onion
1 stalk of celery	2 mushrooms canned, or 1 fresh mushroom
Parsley	
⅓ pound of lean beef	

Chop these ingredients together and put them into a large saucepan with a small piece of butter. Cook until the meat is well browned. Then add one tablespoon of red or white wine. Cook for a few minutes, then add one tablespoon of tomato paste dissolved in a little hot water, or two and one-half tablespoons of the other tomato sauce. Cook well, adding from time to time a little water—one-half cup in all. Wash the rice (a little less than a cupful), add it to the other ingredients in the saucepan, and cook for about twenty minutes, until the rice is soft, adding more water from time to time. Then add two tablespoons of grated Parmesan cheese, mix well, and serve, with more cheese if desired.

Risotto "alla Nostrale"

Take a small piece of onion, slice into small bits, and put into a saucepan with two tablespoons of butter. Cook until onion is browned.

Wash well one-half cup of rice. Put it into the saucepan with the onion, add salt and pepper, and fry until the rice is dry. Then take one and one-half tablespoons of tomato paste, thinned with hot water (or two tablespoons of other tomato sauce), and add to the rice. Little by little add hot water until the rice is cooked through (about one cup of hot water).

Then add grated cheese, Parmesan or Gruyère, one and one-half tablespoons of butter, and mix well over the fire, then serve.

This rice can be served alone or with fried sausages, or with cold chicken, or any left-over meat prepared in the following manner:

Take one and one-half tablespoons of butter in a saucepan. Cut the cold meat into slices, and add them to the butter. Fry well, then take one and one-half tablespoons of tomato paste, thinned in water (or three tablespoons tomato sauce). Add to the meat a little at a time. Simmer for one-half hour, then put into the middle of hot platter, surrounded by rice, and pour this sauce over all. Add a handful of grated Parmesan cheese to the rice.

This preparation of meat can be served with macaroni or corn-meal instead of the rice.

Rice with Butter and Cheese
(Riso in Bianco)

Take one-half cup of rice. Boil in salted water. After twenty minutes of boiling take off the fire and drain. Then put the rice back into a saucepan with three tablespoons of grated cheese (Parmesan) and three tablespoons of butter. Mix well and serve as an entrée, or around a plate of meat.

Rice with Tomatoes

Boil a cup of rice soft in hot water. Shake it now and then, but do not stir it. Drain it, add a little milk in which a beaten egg has been mixed, one teaspoon of butter, and a little pepper and salt. Simmer for five minutes, and if the rice has not absorbed all the milk, drain it again. Put the rice around a dish, smooth it into a wall, wash it over with the yolk of a beaten egg, and put it into the oven until firm. Take the strained juice and pulp of seven or eight tomatoes, season with pepper, a little salt and sugar, and one-half of a chopped-up onion; stew for twenty minutes, then stir in one tablespoon of butter and two tablespoons of fine bread crumbs. Stew three or four minutes to thicken, and then pour the tomatoes into the dish, in the middle of the rice, and serve.

Rice with Tomatoes "all' Indiana"

Wash a cup of rice and boil it. Take seven or eight good-sized tomatoes, boil and strain them, and season with salt and a little allspice. Take a baking-dish and put into it alternate layers of tomato and rice, finishing off with a layer of tomato, covered up with grated bread crumbs moistened with melted butter. Bake in a moderate oven for a good half-hour.

Risotto with Ham

Cut into small pieces one ounce of raw ham, fat and lean. Chop up fine a small piece of onion, and put it with the ham into a frying-pan with one-half a tablespoon of butter. Fry slowly until the ham and onions are golden. Then add one-half cup of uncooked rice; when it has cooked for a few minutes, add twice its height of bouillon (or water), salt and pepper, a dash of nutmeg, and mix well and allow it to boil for twenty minutes over a good fire. Then take off the stove, add two tablespoons of butter and two tablespoons of Parmesan cheese grated; mix well and serve.

Rice with Mushrooms

10 mushrooms if canned, or 5 or 6 if fresh ones   ¾ of a cup of rice

Chop up a little onion, parsley, celery, and carrot together, and put them on the fire with two tablespoons of good olive-oil. When this sauce is colored, add two tablespoons of tomato paste, thinned with hot water (or a corresponding quantity of tomato sauce). Season with salt and pepper. Cut the mushrooms into small pieces, and add them to the sauce. Cook for twenty minutes over a medium fire. Put on one side and prepare the rice as follows:

Fry the rice with a lump of butter until dry; then add hot water, a little at a time, and boil gently. When the rice is half cooked (after about ten minutes) add the mushrooms and sauce, and cook for another ten minutes. Add grated Parmesan cheese before serving.

Polenta
(*Indian Meal*)

¾ of a cup of yellow Indian meal (fine)   3 cups of water

Put the water into a granite or iron saucepan, add salt. When it begins to boil add the Indian meal, little by little. Keep stirring constantly as you pour it in, to prevent lumps. Boil for one-half hour, stirring constantly over a moderate fire. If desired, a little more water may be added if preferred not so thick. Add grated cheese and butter.

Polenta Fritters

Put one pinch of salt and one tablespoon of sugar into a cup of milk, and put it on to boil. As soon as it boils pour in, little by little, one-half scant cup of fine Indian meal, stirring constantly with a wooden spoon. Allow it to boil gently for twenty minutes.

Take it off the stove, add one level tablespoon of butter and the yolk of one egg and a little grated lemon-peel. Beat up well to mix the egg and butter. Then turn the mixture onto the bread-board, which has been dampened; spread it out to the thickness of a finger. Allow it to cool, then cut into squares or diamonds or little rounds, dip these into egg and then into the bread crumbs, and fry them in boiling lard, a few at a time. Sprinkle with sugar, and serve hot.

Polenta "alla Toscana"

2 cups of Indian meal   3 pints of cold water

Put the water on, and when it boils add salt. Then add the Indian meal, little by little, stirring all the time. Allow it to boil over a moderate fire for one-half hour, stirring constantly. When the meal has become quite stiff, take a wooden spoon and dip it into hot water, and with it detach the Indian meal from the side of the saucepan, then hold the saucepan for a moment over the hottest part of the fire, until the Indian meal has become detached from the bottom. Then turn it out onto the bread-board; it should come out whole in a mold. Let it stand a few moments to cool. Then with a wire cut it into slices about the thickness of a finger. Place these slices on a hot platter in a layer; pour over them a good meat gravy and grated cheese; then put on another layer of the polenta, and add more gravy and cheese, and so on, until your polenta is used up.

SIMPLE ITALIAN COOKERY

Polenta with Chopped Sausages

Prepare the Indian meal as in the preceding receipt.

Take four Deerfoot sausages (or two, if a larger variety of sausage), remove the skins, chop fine, then fry in butter. When they are a nice brown add one tablespoon of stock, and two tablespoons of tomato paste thinned with hot water (or a corresponding amount of the tomato sauce).

Cook for fifteen minutes more. Then cut the polenta in slices as in preceding receipt and add the chopped sausages with their sauce and grated cheese, in layers as before.

Chicken with Polenta

Take a small chicken; clean and prepare it. Take a slice of ham fat four fingers wide and one finger long (or one tablespoon of good lard). Chop up very fine with a chopping knife, and put into a good-sized saucepan. Take one-half an onion, a small carrot, a piece of celery, and cut all into very small pieces and add them all to the fat. Then put in the chicken, the salt, pepper, and a pinch of allspice, and cover the saucepan. Cook until the chicken is covered, basting with the grease, and turning the chicken until it is brown on all sides; then add one-third of a glass of red or white wine. When the wine has become absorbed, add one tablespoon of the tomato paste, dissolved in a cup of hot water (or a cup of tomato sauce not too thick). Cook for a few moments more—until the chicken is thoroughly cooked.

Prepare the Indian meal as in receipt for Indian meal, and serve the chicken surrounded by the Indian meal, with the sauce poured over all and grated cheese sprinkled over the Indian meal.

RICE, ETC.

Pigeon may be prepared in the same way as the chicken and served with the Indian meal; or either one may be served instead of the Indian meal with rice, as in receipt for Risotto alla Nostrale; Macaroni, as in receipt for Macaroni with Butter, or Ribbon Macaroni, as in receipt given.

Polenta Pasticciata

¾ of a cup of Indian meal   1 quart of milk

Boil the milk, and add the Indian meal, a little at a time, when milk is boiling, stirring constantly. Cook for one-half an hour, stirring constantly. Add salt just before taking off the fire. The Indian meal should be stiff when finished. Turn it onto the bread-board, and spread it out to the thickness of two fingers. While it is cooking prepare a meat sauce, and a Béchamel sauce as follows:

MEAT SAUCE

Take a small piece of beef, a small piece of ham, fat and lean, one tablespoon of butter, a small piece of onion, a small piece of carrot, a small piece of celery, a pinch of flour, one-half cup of bouillon (or same amount of water), pepper. Cut the meat into small dice; chop up fine together the ham, onion, carrot, and celery. Put these all together with some pepper into a saucepan with the butter, and when the meat is brown, add the pinch of flour, and the bouillon a little at a time (or the water), and cook for about one-half an hour. This sauce should not be strained.

BÉCHAMEL SAUCE

Take one tablespoon of flour, and one tablespoon of butter. Put them into a saucepan and stir with a wooden spoon until they have become a golden-brown color. Then add, a little at a time, one pint of milk; stir constantly until the sauce is as thick as custard, and is white in color. If it grows too thick, a little more milk may be added; or if it is too thin, a tiny lump of butter rolled in flour will thicken it.

Now take the cold Indian meal and cut it into squares about two inches across. Take a baking-dish of medium depth, butter well, then put in a layer of squares of Indian meal close together, to entirely cover the bottom of the dish. Sprinkle over it grated cheese; then pour on the top enough meat sauce to cover the layer (about two tablespoons), then on the top of this add a layer of Béchamel sauce. Then put another layer of the squares of Indian meal, sprinkle with grated cheese as before, add meat sauce, then Béchamel sauce, and continue in this way until the baking-dish is full, having for the top layer the Béchamel sauce. Put the dish into a moderate oven, and bake until it is a golden brown on top.

Polenta Cake
(*Migliaccio di Farina Gialla*)

2 cups of coarse Indian meal
½ cup of raisins
3 tablespoons of lard
½ teaspoon of salt
3 teaspoons of sugar (granulated)

Mix the salt, sugar, and raisins with the Indian meal in a bowl, then pour in boiling water, a little at a time, and stir well with a wooden spoon until you have a stiff paste and no dry meal remains sticking to the bottom of the bowl.

Then take a cake-tin and grease it well with one-

RICE, ETC.

half of the lard. Then turn out the Indian meal into the pan, and even it out with the wooden spoon. Spread on the top of this the rest of the lard, softened slightly so as you can spread it easily. Cook in a slow oven until a golden brown. Serve hot.

Gnocchi of Farina
(Gnocchi di Semolina)

| 1 pint of milk | ½ cup of farina |
| 1 egg | Butter and cheese |

Put the milk on, and when it boils add salt. Take a wooden spoon and, stirring constantly, add the farina little by little. Cook for ten minutes, stirring constantly. Take off the fire and break into the farina one egg; mix very quickly, so that the egg will not have time to set. Spread the farina onto the breadboard about the height of a finger. Allow it to cool, then cut it into squares or diamonds about two or three inches across. Butter well a baking-dish, and put in the bottom a layer of the squares of farina; sprinkle over a little grated Parmesan cheese (or Gruyère), and put here and there a small dab of butter. Then put in another layer of the squares of farina; add cheese and butter as before. Continue in this way until your baking-dish is full, having on the top layer butter and cheese.

Bake in a hot oven until a brown crust forms. Serve in the baking-dish.

Gnocchi of Potato

Take six medium-sized potatoes and put them on to boil in their skins. When they are done, peel them and pass them through a fine colander. Add a little salt. Take one cup of flour, and mix on the breadboard with the potatoes until they form a paste. Roll this paste with the hands into a sausage about the thickness of three fingers. Cut this roll across into pieces about an inch long. Press these pieces lightly with the finger or the handle of the knife, so they will take little cup-shaped forms. Leave these to one side, and put two quarts of salted water on to boil. When it boils add the gnocchi a few at a time, until all are in the water. When the gnocchi rise to the surface of the water, take them out with the skimmer. Put them into a platter a few at a time, adding each time gravy and cheese, and covering them well. Put a layer of grated cheese sprinkled on top. Serve with meat, or as a first course.

Gnocchi of Milk—a Dessert

1 cup of milk
1 level tablespoon of powdered starch
2 tablespoons of sugar
2 or 3 drops of vanilla extract
2 yolks of eggs

Put all these ingredients together into a saucepan and mix together with a wooden spoon for a few moments. Then put onto the back of the stove where it is not too hot, and cook until the mixture has become stiff. Cook a few moments longer, stirring always; then turn out onto a bread-board and spread to a thickness of a finger and a half. When cold, cut into diamonds or squares the width of two fingers. Butter a baking-dish, and put the squares into it overlapping each other. Add a few dabs of butter here and there. Put another layer of the squares in the dish, more dabs of butter, and so on until the dish is full. Brown in the oven.

SAUCES

Roux for Sauces

Roux is necessary to thicken and give body to sauces. Put one tablespoon of flour and one of butter into a saucepan and cook until the flour has lost any raw taste. Then put the saucepan on the back of the stove and add slowly the stock or milk, one cup for every tablespoon of butter or flour, and stir until smooth. For white sauces take care the flour does not color; for dark sauces let it brown, but take care it does not burn.

Agro Dolce Sauce

Take two tablespoons of sugar (brown or white), one-half a cup of currants, a quarter of a bar of grated chocolate, one tablespoon of chopped candied orange, one of lemon-peel, one of capers, and one cup of vinegar. Mix well together and let soak for two hours; pour it over venison or veal, and simmer for ten minutes.

Béchamel Sauce No. 1

Put two ounces of butter and two tablespoons of flour into a saucepan and stir for five minutes. Pour one and one-half pints of boiling milk gradually in, beating well with a whisk. Add some nutmeg, a few peppercorns, a pinch of salt, and some chopped mushrooms. Cook for one-quarter of an hour, and rub through a fine sieve.

Béchamel Sauce No. 2

Mix three tablespoons of butter and three of flour to a smooth paste, put some peppercorns, one-half an onion, one-half a carrot sliced, a small piece of mace, two teacups of white stock, a pinch of salt and of grated nutmeg, in a stew-pan; simmer for one-half an hour, stirring often, then add one teacup of cream; boil at once, and strain and serve.

Tomato Sauce No. 1

Take ten fresh tomatoes, remove the skins, cut them up; put them into a saucepan and boil them until soft. Then pass them through a sieve. Put their juice into a saucepan with one heaping tablespoon of butter or one-half tablespoon of good lard, salt and pepper, and boil again, adding water if the sauce becomes too thick. This sauce can be kept in a bottle for several days. It can be used for macaroni, etc., in place of the tomato paste.

Tomato Sauce No. 2

Mince one-quarter of an onion, one-half a stalk of celery, a few leaves of sweet basil, and a bunch of parsley up fine. Add one-half cup of olive-oil, a pinch of salt and one of pepper, and cut eight or nine tomatoes into slices. Boil until the sauce is as thick as cream, stirring occasionally, then strain through a sieve and serve.

Tomato Sauce No. 3

Take four pounds of tomatoes, cut them in two, and put them into a two-quart saucepan with two wineglasses of water, two saltspoons of salt, one of pepper, cover the saucepan, and boil for forty minutes, stirring often to prevent burning; then strain. Make

SAUCES

a roux in another saucepan with one ounce of butter and three-quarters of an ounce of flour. Cook for three minutes, mixing well. Take roux off the fire, and pour the tomatoes into it a little at a time, stirring to keep it smooth. Add two wineglasses of stock, put on the fire, and cook for twenty minutes, stirring all the time.

Butter Sauce

Take eight ounces of butter, one tablespoon of salt, one of pepper, and two tablespoons of lemon juice. Stir with a wooden spoon over the fire until the butter is half melted, then take it off and continue to stir until it is quite liquid. By taking the butter off the stove before it is all melted it will have a pleasant taste of fresh cream; this is all lost otherwise.

Lombarda Sauce

Put two tumblers of white roux and one of chicken jelly into a saucepan, reduce, and add three yolks of eggs mixed with two ounces of butter and the juice of one-half lemon. Before it boils take the saucepan off the fire, and add one tumbler of thick tomato sauce (see Sauces, page 30), strain, and just before serving add one tablespoon of sweet herbs minced fine.

"Alla Panna" Sauce

Melt one-half a pound of butter, add a little flour, salt, pepper, and grated nutmeg. Stir until thick, then add one pint of cream, a little chopped parsley, and heat for five minutes.

Meat Sauce

Put into a saucepan one pound of beef and one-half an onion chopped up with three ounces of lard, some

SIMPLE ITALIAN COOKERY

parsley, salt, pepper, one clove, and a very small slice of ham. Fry these over a hot fire for a few moments, moving them continually, and when the onion is browned add four tablespoons of red wine, and four tablespoons of tomato sauce (or tomato paste). When this sauce begins to sputter, add, little by little, some boiling water. Stick a fork into the meat from time to time to allow the juices to escape. Take a little of the sauce in a spoon, and when it looks a good golden color, and there is a sufficient quantity to cover the meat, put the covered saucepan at the back of the stove and allow it to simmer until the meat is thoroughly cooked. Then take out the meat, slice it, prepare macaroni, or any paste you desire, and serve it with the meat, and the sauce poured over all, and the addition of butter and grated cheese.

Economical Sauce

Take one-half of an old onion and chop it up fine. Take one small carrot, wash it, scrape it, and cut it into transverse slices; do the same with a stalk of celery, some parsley, and one fresh or canned mushroom. Then take a slice of ham (raw if possible), fat and lean, about four fingers wide and one finger high. Chop it up fine, and put it into a medium-sized saucepan with one tablespoon of butter. When the ham is colored, put in the chopped-up vegetables, one clove, salt, and pepper, and stir constantly, allowing the vegetables to cook thoroughly but not to burn, which will destroy the taste of the sauce. It should be a golden color. A little red wine may be added if you have it, but this is not necessary. Then add four fresh tomatoes, cut into several pieces, the skins removed, and the seeds taken out. Allow these to cook

SAUCES

in the sauce until they sputter, then add a little water (or bouillon if you have it), allow it to boil for a few moments more, then take it off the fire and pass it through a sieve or fine colander, pressing hard so that all will pass through. If it is too thick after straining, add water or bouillon, and put it back and allow it to boil again a few moments. This sauce can be used for macaroni, gnocchi, left-over meat, egg, etc. The success of the sauce depends upon the proper frying of the onion in it.

Hot Piquante Sauce

Chop up fine two ounces of lean ham and a small piece of onion, add a little celery, the stalks of parsley, one clove, one-half tablespoon of pepper, and one-half bay-leaf. Pour over these ingredients a scant one-half cup of vinegar. Cover the saucepan and allow it to boil until it has consumed one-half. Put into another saucepan one-half cup of bouillon (or water in which you have dissolved one tablespoon of extract of beef). Allow it to boil, and then thicken with a teaspoon of potato flour which has been diluted in a little cold water. Drop this, little by little, into the saucepan until you have gained the required thickness for the sauce. Then pour in the boiled vinegar, passing it through cheese-cloth. Mix well together and add a teaspoon of French mustard, some capers, and some chopped-up pickles. Serve hot with meats or tongue. The pepper should predominate in this sauce.

Piquante Sauce with Egg

Take some anchovy paste — one tablespoon, two tablespoons of chopped parsley, some capers and chopped pickles, one teaspoon of French mustard, and the yolks of two hard-boiled eggs. Work this all together into a paste, then add three tablespoons of olive-oil and two or three of vinegar and a pinch of salt and pepper. This sauce is good with both meat and fish.

EGGS

Eggs with Peas

Take one and one-half cups of green peas, and cook them with one and one-half tablespoons of good butter, and a pinch of salt. Take four hard-boiled eggs, cut them in two lengthwise, and put them on a platter; pour over them the peas as a sauce.

Eggs "alla Milanese"

Hard boil four eggs, cut them in four pieces each, put them in a platter, and pour over them the following sauce:

CREAM OF LEMON SAUCE

Take one cup of cold water, and pour one-half of it in a bowl with one tablespoon of starch, stir well until starch is dissolved. Pour the other one-half onto one heaping tablespoon of powered sugar and boil for a few moments—until sugar is thoroughly dissolved. Allow it to cool, and then add the starch, and one cup of milk, a pinch of salt, a little grated lemon-rind, and two yolks of eggs. Mix all thoroughly, then strain through a sieve, then put on the stove again, and over a moderate fire, stir it constantly, always in the same direction, until it has assumed the thickness you desire.

Eggs "alla Sciarmante"

Hard boil four eggs; cut into several pieces. Then prepare the following:

Boil down to a syrup one heaping tablespoon of sugar, rind of one-quarter of lemon, one scant cup of water, and a little piece of cinnamon. Then remove the lemon-rind and the cinnamon, and add one cup of milk or cream. When heated through, take off of fire, and add the yolks of four eggs, beating well together. Then pour the sauce over the hard-boiled eggs in a shallow baking-dish, put it in a very moderate oven, and bake. Before serving squeeze on a little lemon juice and garnish with squares of fried bread.

Eggs with Piquante Sauce

Chop up fine one pickled pepper, one teaspoon of capers, one-half small pickled onion and one pickle, and some parsley. Dissolve in boiling water one tablespoon of butter, add the juice of one-half of lemon, a pinch of flour to give a little body, and the chopped pickles. If too sour add some sugar.

Hard boil four eggs, cut them in four, and pour over them the sauce.

Eggs "alla Monachile"

Hard boil four eggs, divide them in half, and pour over them the following sauce: Put two tablespoons of vinegar into a saucepan and one tablespoon of sugar (brown or white), fifteen almonds chopped up fine, and a small piece of candied citron. Let it boil for a little while, then add a pinch of cinnamon, cloves, pepper, and salt, and if too acid add a little water.

Before taking off the stove add a little flour to give body to the sauce. Pour over the eggs and serve.

Eggs "alla Fiorentina"

Hard boil four eggs. Let them cool in a bowl of cold water. Peel them and divide them in half. Take

EGGS

the yolks and mix with them one heaping tablespoon of butter, one tablespoon of Parmesan cheese grated, and a little salt and pepper. Put this mixture into a saucepan with the yolks of two raw eggs, and one-half of the white of one egg. Stir well until the mixture becomes thick. Then fill the hard-boiled whites of the eggs with the stuffing; if any stuffing remains over, spread it on the platter under the eggs. Then put one-half cup of milk in a saucepan with one-half tablespoon of butter and one-half tablespoon of flour, salt, and pepper. Boil for a few moments, stirring well, then pour over the eggs, sprinkle well with grated Parmesan cheese, and put in the oven and brown.

Lightning Omelette

Butter a baking-dish and put in the bottom of it slices of stale bread (brown bread is better than white) which have been dipped in milk. Then put in a layer of very thin slices of Gruyère cheese. Take two eggs, beat them up to a froth, add salt and pepper, pour them into a baking-dish on top of the bread and cheese, then put it in the oven until it is browned on top. Serve hot.

Eggs "alla Piacentina"

Take the whites of four eggs, and beat until stiff. Then add the yolks and one rounded tablespoon of melted butter, and a little salt and pepper. Take a small baking-dish, butter it well, and put in the bottom a layer or two of very thin slices of cheese, Parmesan or Gruyère. Put into the oven for a few moments until thoroughly heated, then pour on the whites of eggs mixed with the other ingredients, put back in the oven, and serve when the eggs are a golden brown.

Eggs "alla Benedettina"

Roast two small peppers, take off their skins, remove the seeds, and cut into strips. Take two tomatoes (not too ripe), boil them, remove the skins and seeds, and cut into thin strips also. Then wash two anchovies, remove the bones, and cut also into strips. Take a small baking-dish, put in the strips of peppers and tomatoes and the anchovies. Add two tablespoons of good olive-oil and put on the top of the stove until the ingredients boil. Then break into the dish four eggs, taking care to keep the yolks whole. Add salt and pepper, and put the dish into the oven until the eggs are cooked.

Eggs "alla Romana"

Beat four eggs, whites and yolks together. Add one tablespoon of milk or cream, salt and pepper, one tablespoon of grated Parmesan cheese, and a little chopped-up parsley. With this make three or four omelettes about the thickness of a ten-cent piece. As the omelettes are finished lay them on a napkin to cool; then cut them transversely into strips about one-quarter of an inch wide. Then put the strips into a saucepan with some heated butter. Heat them through thoroughly and serve with grated cheese and the following meat sauce poured over them:

MEAT SAUCE

Chop up some ham fat with a little onion, celery, carrot, and parsley. Add a small piece of beef and cook until beef is well colored. Then add one and one-half tablespoons of red wine (or white), cook until wine is absorbed, then add one tablespoon of tomato paste diluted with water, or four fresh tomatoes, and boil fifteen minutes.

FISH

Codfish "alla Giardiniera"

Take one pound of salted codfish, boil it, remove the skin and bones, and shred it. Then take one good carrot, one-half a turnip, scrape them, cut them into slices, and boil them for a few moments. Then drain off the water, and put them into a saucepan with one and one-half tablespoons of butter and finish cooking them, adding from time to time a little boiling water. When the vegetables are cooked add the codfish, mix well, and serve.

Codfish with Egg Sauce

Take one pound of salt codfish. Boil it and remove the skin and bones. Then fry lightly in butter, adding chopped-up parsley, salt, and pepper. Stir about constantly, and add from time to time a little boiling water, until the fish is thoroughly cooked. Then beat up the yolks of two eggs and add them with a little flour, and cook for a few moments more. Squeeze on some lemon juice and serve.

Codfish "alla Marinaia"

Take one pound of salt codfish. Boil slightly until you can remove the skin and bones. Chop up fine a piece of onion, and parsley, and fry them in a saucepan with three tablespoons of best olive-oil, then put in the codfish with salt, pepper, and a pinch of allspice.

While this is cooking, put into another saucepan three tablespoons of best vinegar, two tablespoons of fish broth, and one-half bay-leaf. Add a little flour to give body to the sauce, stir well, then remove the bay-leaf, and take the saucepan off the fire. Arrange the platter with pieces of fried bread in a layer on the bottom, then the codfish, and then the sauce poured over it.

Fresh Codfish "al Vino Bianco"

Remove the bones from three-quarters of a pound of fresh codfish. Cut into slices lengthwise. Butter a baking-dish, put in the fish, put more butter on top of it, salt and pepper, and one-half glass of dry white wine. Cook for twenty minutes in a hot oven, then place the fish on a platter, take the juice left over in the baking-dish, put it into a saucepan, add a little flour, some more butter, and the juice of half a lemon. Before taking off the fire, add some chopped-up parsley, and then pour the sauce over the fish, and serve.

Codfish with Green Peppers

Take one-half pound of salted codfish which has been soaked to remove the saltiness. Remove the skin and bones, and cut the codfish into small squares. Then dip it again into fresh water, and put the squares onto a napkin to dry. The fish may either be left as it is, or before proceeding, you may roll it in flour and fry it in lard or oil.

Then take two good-sized green peppers, roast them on top of the stove, remove the skins and seeds, wash them, dry them, and cut them in narrow strips. When this is done put three generous tablespoons of olive-oil into a saucepan with one onion cut up small, and fry the onion over a slow fire.

FISH

Take two big tomatoes, skin them, remove the seeds and hard parts, and cut them into small pieces. When the onion has taken a good color, add the tomatoes, and cook until they sputter, then add the peppers and a little salt and pepper. If the sauce is too thick add a little water. When the peppers are half cooked, add some chopped-up parsley and the codfish. Cover up the saucepan and let it simmer until the fish is cooked.

This dish is also good cold.

VEGETABLES

Onions "alla Parmegiana"

Take six onions. Take out the centers with an apple-corer and fill them up with the following stuffing: One tablespoon of grated Parmesan cheese mixed with two hard-boiled eggs and chopped parsley. Boil them first, then roll them in flour and fry them in olive-oil or butter. Then put them in a baking-dish with one-half tablespoon of grated Parmesan cheese and one tablespoon of melted butter. Put them in the oven and bake until golden.

Onions "alla Veneziana"

Take six small onions, remove the centers with an apple-corer. Boil them for a few moments, drain them, and stuff them with the following: Take a piece of bread, dip it in milk, squeeze out the milk, and mix the bread with one tablespoon of grated Parmesan cheese, the yolks of two hard-boiled eggs. Mix well together, then add some fine-chopped parsley, a pinch of sugar, salt and pepper, and the yolk of one raw egg; mix again well, and then stuff the onions with the mixture. Then dip them in flour and in egg, and fry them in lard. Put them on a platter and serve with a piquante sauce, made as follows: Chop up fine some pickles, capers, and pickled pepper, and add one-half cup of water. When these are cooked, add one tablespoon of butter and cook a little while longer, then pour over the onions and serve.

VEGETABLES

Lima Beans with Ham

Take three-quarters of a pound of lima beans, very tender young ones. Put them in boiling water for about five minutes to whiten them. Then put into a saucepan one heaping tablespoon of butter, some chopped parsley, and one small onion chopped up fine. When the onion is fried, add three ounces of raw ham, also chopped up. When the ham is fried put in the lima beans, and a little while before they are cooked add two or three tablespoons of stock. Serve with dice of fried bread.

Fried Squash, Parsnips, Celery, and Mushrooms

Take two small squash, the smallest size possible; cut off the two ends, divide them in two, and slice them in fine slices lengthwise. Put them in an earthen dish and sprinkle well with salt. Take one parsnip, scrape it, wash it, and boil it slightly, slice it, add it to the squash with more salt. Take the heart of celery, boil for a moment, and slice as with the other vegetables. Lastly, take some mushrooms, not very large ones, clean them, boil them a moment, and add them to the rest. Then dry all the vegetables with a clean towel, mix them all together, roll them thoroughly in flour, dip in egg, and fry in hot lard, dropping them in carelessly. Serve them in a hot dish with a napkin under them.

Pumpkin "alla Parmegiana"

Take a slice of pumpkin, remove the rind and the seeds, cut into square pieces, and then slice these into slivers about the thickness of a ten-cent piece. Boil these for a moment in salted water, drain and put them into a saucepan, and fry in butter, with a little salt and a pinch of allspice. Serve with grated Parmesan cheese and melted butter. Or, if preferred, when the pumpkin is fried, put it in a baking-dish, add thin slices of cheese (Parmesan or Gruyère), and put it into the oven until browned.

Fried Pumpkin

Take a slice of pumpkin, remove the rind and the seeds. Cut it into strips as for French fried potatoes, only finer. Roll in flour and dip in egg, and fry in boiling lard or olive-oil.

If desired as garnishing for meat, cut the pumpkin exceedingly fine, roll in flour, but not in egg, and fry.

Spinach "alla Romana"

Clean and prepare the spinach. Put one pint of cold water with one tablespoon of salt on to boil, and when it boils put in the spinach. When the spinach is cooked—in about ten minutes—drain it in a colander, and turn onto it the cold water from the faucet for a few moments. Then squeeze out all the water with the hands. Put three tablespoons of olive-oil into a frying-pan; when this is thoroughly hot add the spinach, salt, and pepper. Cook for a few moments, stirring well with a fork and spoon, so the oil will permeate the spinach; then serve. Do not chop the spinach.

Spinach Soufflé

Wash the spinach in several waters, put it in a covered saucepan on a good fire. Stir now and then to prevent burning, and after fifteen minutes add one tablespoon of salt. Cook five minutes more; drain and squeeze out the water. Then chop up very fine. Put into a saucepan one generous tablespoon of butter, three-quarters tablespoon of flour, stir, and

VEGETABLES

when they are half cooked, add the spinach and a little salt and pepper. Cook for five minutes, then pour in four or five tablespoons of cream, stirring constantly to prevent burning. Take a cup of spinach, prepared as above, beat up the yolk of one egg, mix it with the spinach, and stir over the fire until the egg is set; then let it cool, and before serving stir the well-beaten whites of three eggs lightly into it. Fill china cups or buttered papered forms half full, put them into a hot oven for ten or fifteen minutes, and serve at once. If too little baked or not served at once, the soufflé will be spoiled.

Spinach "in Riccioli"

Boil the spinach and pass it through a fine colander. Beat up two eggs, add salt and pepper, and mix enough spinach into them to make them green. Put a little olive-oil into a frying-pan, and when it is thoroughly heated (but not boiling), pour a little of the egg, turning the pan about so that the pancake should be as thin as a piece of paper and dry. Toss if necessary. Take it out; repeat with the rest of the egg. Then take the pancakes, place them one on top of the other, and cut them into pieces the width of a finger and about two inches long. Fry them in butter, and grate a little Parmesan cheese over them. They make a very nice garnish.

Spinach in a Mold with Mushrooms

Boil the spinach for a few moments, drain, squeeze out the water, then pound it well, and pass it through a fine colander. Put it into a saucepan with a lump of butter and a few drops of lemon juice. Let it boil for a few moments, then turn it into a dish and allow it to cool. When cold mix with it the beaten-up yolks of two eggs. Put them into a buttered mold, leaving an empty space in the middle. Bake in a slow oven for about an hour. When cooked turn it out onto a dish, and fill up the empty space with mushrooms, which you have prepared as follows: Wash and clean a sufficient quantity of mushrooms and put them into a saucepan with a good-sized lump of butter, a little flour, salt, and pepper. Cook over a brisk fire for ten minutes. Moisten well with chicken broth or stock, and add some roux made as follows: Put one tablespoon of flour and one of butter into a saucepan, and cook until the flour has lost all raw taste. Then add stock or milk as desired, slowly — one cup for every tablespoon of butter or flour — and stir until smooth. Squeeze the juice of half a lemon on the mushrooms, put them with their sauce into the spinach, and serve.

Flan of Vegetables

Wash, chop up fine, and boil several vegetables, a potato, some spinach, a carrot, and a small beet, etc., then boil them again in a saucepan with some stock; then add a half a cup of cream or milk, stir well together, take them off the stove, and let them cool. When cool add the yolks of two eggs, some grated cheese, and the whites of the eggs beaten up. Put the vegetables into a mold which has been well buttered and lined with bread crumbs, and cook in the oven.

Lettuce in the Oven

Take several young lettuces, wash them and remove their wilted leaves, tie the tops together, and lay the lettuces side by side in a baking-pan and pour in one and one-half inches of stock. Cover the pan, and put it in a moderate oven for one-half an hour, adding stock when necessary. Place a fork under the middle of each lettuce, raise and drain, and lay them doubled up on a hot dish. Season the gravy in the pan with butter, salt, and pepper, thicken with one beaten egg, and pour it over the lettuce. Serve hot.

Cucumbers "alla Toscana"

Peel and blanch three or four cucumbers in boiling salted water for five minutes. Drain and cut them into pieces one inch thick and put them into a frying-pan with one ounce of butter, a little flour, and one-half pint of veal broth, stir well, and add some salt and pepper. Reduce for about fifteen minutes, stirring until it boils, add one teaspoon of chopped parsley, one-half a teaspoon of grated nutmeg, one-half a cup of cream, and the beaten-up yolks of two eggs. Put on the fire again for three or four minutes. Do not let boil, and serve hot.

Cauliflower "in Stufato"

Remove the outer leaves and clean a fine cauliflower. Cut it into several pieces and wash them well with cold water, put them into a pot of boiling salted water, and cook quickly for twenty or thirty minutes, until they are quite tender. Take them out without breaking, and place them on pieces of buttered toast, then put some butter in a frying-pan, add a little flour mixed with some stock, stir well until it boils, then add several finely chopped mushrooms, and cook a little more. Take it off the fire, and add the yolks of two eggs which have been well beaten, salt, pepper, grated nutmeg, and the juice of one lemon. Pour this sauce over and round the cauliflower, and serve. The sauce must not be boiled after adding the eggs.

Celery Fried

Cut off the green leaves, and cut the stalks of the celery in pieces about an inch long. Wash them and then put them into boiling water for fifteen minutes. Then dry on a napkin. Beat up an egg with a little stock, or hot water, add salt and pepper, dip the celery in, then roll it in bread crumbs, and fry in boiling lard.

Celery with Tomato Sauce

Cut off the green leaves, clean and wash the celery stalks, and then throw them into boiling water and boil fast for twenty minutes. Drain, dry well, put them on a dish, and pour a pint of tomato sauce, or tomato paste diluted with hot water, over them.

Tomatoes "alla Piemontese"

Take four rather unripe tomatoes of about the same size, put them into boiling water and boil for a few minutes. Cut off the stem part, and take out some of the inside with as many seeds as you can. Fill them with boiled rice and some mushrooms chopped up small. Pour over them the yolks of two eggs, place them in the oven to color; serve hot.

Tomatoes "alla Spagnuola"

Take three or four large ripe tomatoes and boil them. Lay them on a sieve to drain until wanted, and then pass them through a fine hair-sieve. Put them in a stew-pan and stir until all the liquid is evaporated. Then add a small piece of butter and three or four raw eggs, stirring them quickly with the tomatoes. When the eggs are cooked, turn all out into a dish and serve hot.

VEGETABLES

Tomatoes with Eggs

Choose round tomatoes of about equal size and peel them. Cut off their tops, take out their insides, and drop a raw egg into each, replacing the top as cover. Put the tomatoes in a baking-dish and bake for about ten minutes, until the eggs are set. Serve up in the baking-dish very hot, with Béchamel sauce (see Sauces, page 29), or some brown gravy.

Tomato Pudding

Scald, peel, and slice eight tomatoes. Squeeze out three-quarters of their juice into a bowl through cheesecloth, and put it to one side; then chop up the pulp of the tomatoes with two tablespoons of bread crumbs, a little salt, sugar, and pepper, and a tablespoon of melted butter. Pour them in a buttered mold, place the mold in a double boiler, and put on the cover, and boil hard for one hour. Then turn out on a dish. Meanwhile take the juice of the tomatoes, season with sugar, salt, and pepper, mix in one tablespoon of butter rolled in flour. Boil one minute, then pour over the pudding and serve.

String-beans "in Fricassea"

Cut off the ends and string some young string-beans. Cook them in salted water, then drain them well. Put them in a saucepan with some butter, parsley, and chopped onion. Be careful to add occasionally some broth if the beans dry up before they are completely cooked. Boil slowly, and a few moments before taking them off the fire add the yolks of one or two eggs (according to the quantity of beans) well beaten up with a little water, the juice of a lemon, and some grated Parmesan cheese. Stir from time to time,

SIMPLE ITALIAN COOKERY

and never allow them to boil, or the eggs will set. To keep the beans a good color put a pinch of soda into the water with the salt.

String-beans with Tomatoes

Take some young string-beans, cut off the ends, and string them. Wash them in cold water, drain, and while still wet put them into a baking-dish with some good olive-oil, some chopped onion and parsley, salt, and pepper. Put the dish on the fire with its cover on, and cook slowly. As the beans dry add the juice of some tomatoes, or some good tomato conserve. Take care they do not burn.

Fried Bread with Raisins

Take some rather stale bread, cut it into slices, removing the crust. Fry the bread in lard, and then arrange it on a platter; meanwhile prepare the raisins as follows: Take a small saucepan and put into it two tablespoons of good raisins, a good slice of raw ham chopped into small pieces, and a leaf of sage, also chopped up, one tablespoon of granulated sugar, and two tablespoons of good vinegar. Put these ingredients on the fire, and as soon as you have a syrup (stir constantly) pour the raisins onto the pieces of fried bread, and the sauce over and around them. Served with cold meat these are very nice.

MEATS

Fried Sweetbreads, Croquettes, Liver, Etc.
(*Fritto Misto alla Romana*)

Golden Bread, Brains, Sweetbreads, Croquettes of Chicken and Veal and Eggs, Calf's Liver and Pumpkin — all these different ingredients should be fried each in its own manner as follows, a small quantity of each, and served all together on one platter with slices of lemon.

Golden Bread

Choose bread which is elastic, but has no holes in it. Remove the crust and cut it in slices about one inch thick, and from these slices cut little pieces about three inches long and about one inch wide. Trim them off well, so they will not be ragged or uneven. Put these pieces into a bowl and throw on them some boiling water, then remove them immediately and throw them into a big bowl of cold water. This operation should be done quickly, so as to make the bread feel the impression of heat and cold, one directly after the other. Then take the bread between the hands and gently squeeze out the water without breaking the pieces or deforming them. Place them on a napkin to dry. Then dip them in egg which has been beaten up and seasoned with salt and pepper. Allow the egg to soak well into the bread. Fifteen minutes before serving put a frying-pan on with a quantity of lard, and as soon as the lard is lukewarm put in the pieces of bread, turn them as soon as they harden a little on one side. The bread must fry very slowly, and should remain on the fire at least ten minutes, so that the heat can penetrate gradually into the middle and make it light. This bread to be successful should be hollow inside like a fritter when finished. When the bread has taken a good golden color, remove from the lard, drain it on a napkin, add a little salt, and serve very hot.

Sweetbreads

Parboil the sweetbreads, then cook them with one tablespoon of butter and one tablespoon of stock. When cooked cut them into smallish pieces, season with pepper, chopped-up parsley, and one tablespoon of lemon, then roll them in flour; dip into egg and fry.

Fried Brains

Take one lamb's brain, or one-half of a calf's brain, put it in a saucepan with cold water, change the water from time to time for a couple of hours, until the brains are thoroughly cleansed. Then put them in another saucepan with fresh water, and with several pieces of onion, a little salt, a little vinegar (one tablespoon to each brain), and some parsley stems. As soon as the water boils, take the saucepan off, remove the brains, and put them onto a napkin. Cut them into four pieces, put these pieces onto a plate, and season with a little olive-oil, some lemon juice, and chopped parsley. When you are ready to fry, roll in flour, dip in egg, and fry the brain over a moderate fire for seven or eight minutes in olive-oil, lard, or butter.

MEATS

Calf's Liver Fried

Remove the skin, and cut into slices large but thin, roll in flour, dip in egg, and fry in boiling lard, allowing them to remain in the frying-pan only a couple of minutes; then drain on a napkin, sprinkle on a little salt, and serve.

Polenta Croquettes

Boil one-half cup of corn-meal rather hard, and before removing from the fire add a piece of butter and a little grated cheese and mix well. Take it then by spoonfuls and let it fall onto a marble-top table, or a bread-pan which has been wet a little with cold water. These spoonfuls should form little balls about the size of a hen's egg. On each of these croquettes place a very thin slice of Gruyère cheese, so that the cheese will adhere to the corn-meal. Then allow them to cool, and when cold dip into egg, then into bread crumbs, and fry in boiling lard.

Egg Croquettes

Hard boil two eggs, remove the shells, dry them, and cut the eggs in minute pieces. Put one tablespoon of butter into a saucepan, and when it is melted add one and one-half tablespoons of flour; stir constantly for a few moments over a slow fire with a wooden spoon, taking care that the flour does not color. Then pour in one-third of a cup of milk, in which you have put salt and pepper. Cool this sauce for eight or ten minutes, stirring continually to make it smooth, then remove from the fire, put in the chopped-up egg, some parsley chopped fine, and one-half tablespoon of grated Parmesan cheese. When you have mixed these ingredients well together, spread them out on a plate or marble and allow to cool. When this has become cold and hardened, with a wooden spoon divide it into little portions about the size of a nut. Take these and roll them in dried bread crumbs and a little flour. Roll them all then, one at a time, with a rotary motion, and then elongate the balls until they are the shape of ordinary corks, then dip the croquettes into the egg, one at a time, then into bread crumbs again, and a few moments before serving fry in boiling lard. As soon as they are colored remove them immediately from the lard, otherwise they will break to pieces.

Polenta Fritters, Fried Pumpkin, Fried Squash, and Parsnips may also be added or substituted if desired.

Little Filets "alla Napolitana"

Butter well a frying-pan, and sprinkle over the bottom a piece of lean ham (raw if possible) chopped up fine. Then a layer of mushrooms chopped fine, then a layer of minced parsley. The bottom of the pan should be entirely covered with these three ingredients. Then from a filet of beef cut some little slices, about one-half an inch thick and round in shape. Put these in the frying-pan, one piece near the other, so the bottom shall be covered. Sprinkle on salt and pepper, and put it on the fire. When the filets are cooked on one side, turn them over on the other, but with care, so the ingredients at the bottom of the pan will stick to the meat. When the filets are cooked on both sides, squeeze on the juice of half a lemon, and add a little meat stock. Put the filets on a platter, and pour over them their sauce, and serve with croutons (fried bread).

Involtini of Beef "alla Siciliana"

Take three-quarters of a pound of beef, two ounces of ham, one tablespoon of butter (or one-half table-

MEATS

spoon of lard), some bread, some parsley, and a piece of onion. Chop up the onion fine and put it in a saucepan with the butter (or lard). When it is colored, put in the parsley and the ham cut up into little pieces, at the same time add the bread cut up into three or four small dice, salt, pepper, and a dash of nutmeg. Mix all together well. Cut the meat into six slices, pound them to flatten out; salt slightly, and when the other ingredients are cooked, put a portion on each slice of meat. Then roll up the meat like sausages, put them on skewers, alternating with a piece of fried bread of the same size. Butter well, roll in fresh bread crumbs, and broil on the gridiron over a slow fire. These are nice served with salad.

Polpettone "alla Napolitana"

Take three-quarters of a pound of lean beef without skin or bones from the rump-steak, flatten it out with a knife in a manner to widen it without tearing the meat. Salt and pepper it. Then take one and one-half ounces of ham, fat and lean, and chop it up fine with a little piece of onion, some parsley, and some thyme, then add twice its volume of fresh bread crumbs (which have been dipped in water and squeezed out). When the bread has been well mixed add the yolk of one egg and mix again well, spread this mixture all over the surface of the beef, leveling it off with a knife. Then sprinkle on a few raisins, and then roll up the meat like a cigar, but bigger in the middle than at the ends. Tie it up then, crosswise and lengthwise, and brown it in a saucepan with a little lard and some ham. As soon as it colors add some chopped-up pieces of onion, celery, carrot, and one clove. When these vegetables are cooked add several pieces of tomato, and let the meat simmer for about two hours, basting it now and then. When the meat is cooked remove the string, place the polpettone on a platter, strain the sauce through a sieve, pour it over the meat, and serve.

Bocconcini

Cut up the meat, lamb, veal, mutton, or fresh pork into pieces about two inches wide. Sprinkle on salt and pepper and put them aside. Then cut an equal number of pieces of bread about one-half inch thick, and a little bit bigger then the pieces of meat. Next cut pieces of ham, fat and lean, the same size as the pieces of meat, but double the number. Then take a skewer (or two if one is not sufficient), and put on it first a piece of bread, then a piece of ham, then a leaf of sage, then one of the pieces of meat, then another leaf of sage, then the ham, then the bread, and so on in this order, having always the meat between two leaves of sage, two slices of ham, and two pieces of bread. Coat everything well, and especially the bread, with olive-oil or melted butter, and then broil them over a hot fire for a good one-quarter of an hour, turning them constantly until they are colored a golden brown and are crisp. If preferred, these can be cooked in the oven. Put them on several wooden skewers, and lay them in a pan and cook until brown and crisp. Serve with lettuce salad.

Meat with Ribbon Macaroni

Take a piece of ham fat, one finger high and four fingers wide, chop up fine with a piece of onion, piece of celery, piece of carrot, and put into a saucepan. Take three-quarters of a pound of meat, either lamb, veal, beef, or fresh pork, cut it into several pieces,

MEATS

salt and pepper it, and put a pinch of allspice, then put it into the saucepan; cook it until it is well colored, then add two tablespoons of red or white wine. When it is absorbed add one tablespoon of tomato paste, dissolved in water, or tomato sauce of fresh tomatoes (receipt Tomato Sauce No. 1). Cook over a moderate fire, one hour longer if the meat is veal or lamb, and one and one-half hours to two hours for pork or beef, adding water if necessary.

This meat can be served with Ribbon Macaroni. Put the meat in the middle, the macaroni around it, and the sauce over all, adding two tablespoons of grated Parmesan cheese to the macaroni after it is boiled, and mixing well before putting it on the platter. Sprinkle on a little more cheese before carrying to the table.

This dish can be made equally well with left-over meats of any kind, turkey being especially good served this way.

SALADS

Salad "del Prevosto"

Boil in their skins three good-sized potatoes, peel them and slice them, then put them into a salad bowl, and pour over them one-half a glass of white wine. Do this about two or three hours before they are wanted, so the potatoes will have time thoroughly to absorb the wine. From time to time mix them with a fork and spoon to let the wine permeate. A few minutes before the meal make a good French salad dressing, add some pickled peppers cut up, some capers, and some chopped-up parsley, pour on the French dressing, mix up well, and serve.

The Cardinal's Salad

Wash a good lettuce and a bunch of water-cress. Cut a cold boiled beef into strips, add six radishes, two hard-boiled eggs chopped up, and one small sliced cucumber. Arrange the lettuce-leaves in a salad-bowl, mix the other ingredients with a sufficient quantity of mayonnaise sauce, put them in the midst of the lettuce, and serve.

Endive Salad

Take a head of endive, wash it and dry it well, and put it into a salad-bowl. Pour over it three tablespoons of good olive-oil. Mix one tablespoon of

SALADS

honey (or sugar), one of vinegar, and salt and pepper in a cup, and pour over the salad just before serving.

Italian Salad

Cut one carrot and one turnip into slices, and cook them in boiling soup. When cold, mix them with two cold boiled potatoes and one beet cut into strips. Add a very little chopped leeks or onion, pour some sauce, "Lombarda" (see Sauces, page 31), over the salad, and garnish with water-cress.

"Alla Pollastra" Salad

Chop up six lettuce-leaves and three stalks of celery, cut up the remains of a cold fowl in small pieces, and mix with one tablespoon of vinegar and salt and pepper in a salad bowl. Pour a cup of mayonnaise sauce over, and garnish with quarters of hard-boiled egg, one tablespoon of capers, six stoned olives, and some small, tender lettuce-leaves.

"Alla Macedoine" Salad

Cut into small pieces one cold boiled beet and half an onion. Add some cold boiled string-beans, some cold boiled asparagus tips, two tablespoons of cold cooked peas, one cold boiled carrot, and some celery. Mix them together, and pour over all a mayonnaise sauce. Add the juice of a lemon and serve.

DESSERTS

Chestnut Fritters

Take twenty good chestnuts and roast them on a slow fire so that they won't color. Remove the shells without breaking the nuts, and put them into a saucepan with one level tablespoon of powdered sugar and one-half glass of milk and a little vanilla. Cover the saucepan and let it cook slowly (simmer) for more than a half-hour. Then drain the chestnuts and pass them through a sieve. Put them back in a bowl with one-half a tablespoon of butter, the yolks of three eggs, and mix well without cooking. Allow them to cool, and then take a small portion at a time, the size of a nut, roll them, dip them in egg, and in bread crumbs, and fry in butter and lard, a few at a time. Serve hot with powdered sugar.

Chestnuts "alla Lucifero"

Take forty good chestnuts and roast them over a slow fire. Do not allow them to become dried up or colored. Remove the shells carefully, put them in a bowl, and pour over them one-half a glass of rum and two or three tablespoons of powdered sugar. Set fire to the rum and baste the chestnuts constantly as long as the rum will burn, turning the chestnuts

DESSERTS

about so they will absorb the rum and become colored.

Peaches with Wine

Take four very ripe peaches, cut them in two, take out the stones, peel them, and cut them in thin slices. Put them in a bowl and cover them up until wanted. Put in a saucepan one glass of red wine, two tablespoons of powdered sugar, a piece of cinnamon, and a piece of a rind of lemon. Boil these together, and then pour the liquid over the peaches in the bowl while still boiling. Cover the bowl, and allow it to stand for at least two hours. Then turn into the dish in which you will serve the peaches and the wine.

Hot Wine

Put into the saucepan one pint of red or white wine, the first preferred. Add two heaping tablespoons of sugar, a piece of rind of lemon or orange, and a small stick of cinnamon. Put it onto the fire and stir until the sugar is dissolved. When the wine boils, strain it through some cheese-cloth and pour it into glasses, and serve hot.

Milk of Almond Ice

Take one-half pound of almonds. Remove the shells and skins, and put them into a large receptacle of cold water. Add three bitter almonds to the number. Remove them from the water, and pound them up in a bowl, adding from time to time a little water. Then add more water and put them into a cheese-cloth and wring it, to extract all the juices you can. Then pound them some more, adding water, and squeeze out as before. To the milk you have extracted from the almonds add four tablespoons of powdered sugar and one-half tablespoon of orange water; put into the freezer and freeze.

If desired, you can put half the quantity of almonds and the other half of cantaloup seeds, pound together, and proceed in the same manner. This combination is refreshing and delicious.

INDEX

A

Agro Dolce Sauce, 29.
"Alla Macedoine" Salad, 59.
"Alla Panna" Sauce, 31.
"Alla Pollastra" Salad, 59.

B

Béchamel Sauce, 25.
        Sauce No. 1, 29.
        Sauce No. 2, 30.
Beef Soup Stock, 3, 4.
Bocconcini, 56.
Bread, Fried, with Raisins, 50.
        Golden, 51.
Butter Sauce, 31.

C

Calf's Brains, Fried, 52.
        Liver, Fried, 53.
Caramel, for soup stock, 4.
Cardinal's Salad, 58.
Cauliflower "in Stufato," 47.
Celery, Fried, 43, 48.
        with Tomato Sauce, 48.

Chestnut Fritters, 60.
Chestnuts "alla Lucifero," 60.
Chicken, Broth, 4.
 with Polenta, 24.
Codfish, "alla Giardiniera," 39.
 "alla Marinaia," 39, 40.
 "alla Vino Bianco," 40.
 Soup, 5.
 with Egg Sauce, 39.
 with Green Peppers, 40, **41**.
Cream of Lemon Sauce, 35.
Cucumbers "alla Toscana," 47.

D

"Del Prevosta" Salad, 58.
DESSERTS, SECTION ON, 60–62.

E

Economical Sauce, 32, 33.
Egg Croquettes, 53, 54.
 with Piquante Sauce, 33.
EGGS, SECTION ON, 35–40.
Eggs, "alla Benedettina," 38.
 "alla Fiorentina," 36.
 "alla Milanese," 35.
 "alla Monachile," 36.
 "alla Piacentina," 37.
 "alla Romana," 38.
 "alla Sciarmante," 35.
 Lightning Omelette, **37**.
 with Peas, 35.
Endive Salad, 38.

INDEX

F

Filets, little, "alla Napolitana," 54.
Fish Broth, 5.
FISH, SECTION ON, 39–41.
Flan of Vegetables, 46.
Fried Squash, Parsnips, Celery, and Mushrooms, 43.
Fritters, Polenta, 22.
        Chestnut, 60.

G

Gnocchi, of Farina, 27.
       of Milk, 28.
       of Potato, 27.
Golden Bread, 51.

H

Hot Piquante Sauce, 33.
Hot Wine, 61.

I

Indian Meal (Polenta), 22.
Involtini of Beef "alla Siciliana," 54.
Italian Salad, 59.

L

Lamb's Brains, fried, 52.
Lentil Soup, 6.
Lettuce in the Oven, 46.
Lettuce Soup, 7.
Lima Beans with Ham, 43.
Little Filets "alla Napolitana," 54.
Lombarda Sauce, 31.

M

MACARONI AND OTHER PASTES, SECTION ON, 9–17.
Macaroni, "alla San Giovannello," 13.
       Ribbon, 14.
       Sicilian, with Eggplant, 11.
       Timbale of, 16.
       Timbale of Ribbon, 17.
       with Butter and Cheese, 10.
       with Meat and Sauce, 10.
       with Tomato Sauce, 9.
Meat, Sauce, 25, 31, 32, 38.
       with Ribbon Macaroni, 56, 57.
MEATS, SECTION ON, 51–57.
Milk of Almond Ice, 61, 62.
Mushrooms, Fried, 43.
       with Rice, 22.

O

Onions "alla Parmegiana," 42.
    "alla Veneziana," 42.

P

Parsnips, Fried, 43.
Peaches with Wine, 61.
Piquante Sauce with Eggs, 36.
Polenta, "alla Toscana," 23.
       Cake, 26, 27.
       Croquettes, 53.
       Fritters, 22, 23.
       Indian Meal, 22.
       Pasticciata, 25.
       with Chicken, 24.
       with Chopped Sausages, 24.

INDEX

Polpettone "alla Napolitana," 55, 56.
Potato Soup, 8.
Pumpkin, "alla Parmegiana," 43.
       Fried, 44.
       Soup, 7, 8.

R

Ravioli, of Curds and Spinach, 15.
       Sweet, 15.
       with Brains, 15.
       with Bread, 14.
RICE, ETC., SECTION ON, 18-28.
Rice, "alla Nostrale," 19, 20.
    "alla Romana," 19.
    Soup, 4.
    Timbale, 17.
    with Butter and Cheese, 20.
    with Ham, 21.
    with Mushrooms, 22.
    with Peas, 18.
    with Tomatoes, 20, 21.
    with Tomatoes "all' Indiana," 21.
Risotto "alla Nostrale," 19.
       with Ham, 21.
Roux for Sauces, 29.

S

SALADS, SECTION ON, 58-59.
Sauces, Roux for, 29.
SAUCES, SECTION ON, 29-34.
Sausages, Chopped, with Polenta, 24.
SOUPS, SECTION ON, 3-8.
Spaghetti with Tunny-fish, 12.

SIMPLE ITALIAN COOKERY

Spinach, "alla Romana," 44.
    in a mold with Mushrooms, 45, 46.
    "in Riccioli," 45.
    Soufflé, 44, 45.
Squash, Fried, 43.
Stracciatella Soup, 4.
String-beans, "in Fricassea," 49.
    with Tomatoes, 50.
Sweetbreads, Fried, 52.

T

Timbale, of Macaroni, 16.
    of Ribbon Macaroni, 17.
    of Vermicelli with Tomatoes, 13.
Tomato Sauce, 9, 10.
    Sauce No. 1, 30.
    Sauce No. 2, 30.
    Sauce No. 3, 30.
    Pudding, 49.
Tomatoes, "alla Piemontese," 48.
    "alla Spagnuola," 48.
    with Eggs, 49.
    with String-beans, 50.

V

VEGETABLES, SECTION ON, 42–50.
Vegetable, Chowder, 5.
    Soup, 6, 7.
Vermicelli, Timbale of, with Tomatoes, 13.
    with Fish, 12.
    with Olive-oil and Anchovies, 11.
    with Olive-oil, Olives, Capers and Anchovies, 11.

W

Wine, Hot, 61.

THE END